T0397888

MONSTER MANNERS

On the Playground

Written by
Charis Mather

Designed by
Amy Li

Library of Congress Control Number:
2024953022

ISBN
979-8-89359-331-0 (library bound)
979-8-89359-415-7 (paperback)
979-8-89359-386-0 (epub)
979-8-89359-361-7 (hosted ebook)

Printed in the United States of America
Mankato, MN
092025

sales@northstareditions.com
888-417-0195

Written by:
Charis Mather

Edited by:
Rebecca Phillips-Bartlett

Designed by:
Amy Li

American adaptation copyright © 2026 by North Star Editions, Mendota Heights, MN 55120. All rights reserved. No part of this book may be reproduced or utilized in any form or by any means without written permission from the publisher.

On the Playground © 2024 BookLife Publishing
This edition is published by arrangement with BookLife Publishing

All facts, statistics, web addresses and URLs in this book were verified as valid and accurate at time of writing. No responsibility for any changes to external websites or references can be accepted by either the author or publisher.

PHOTO CREDITS
All images are courtesy of Shutterstock.com, unless otherwise specified. With thanks to Getty Images, Thinkstock Photo and iStockphoto.

Recurring – Agafonov Oleg, Omeris. Cover – Archiwiz, mckenna71. P4–5 – billedfab. P6–7; P14–15 – Designsells.

Monsters know many things.

They know how to run and how to jump...

They know how to swim and how to skate...

But there is one thing that many monsters do not know...

MANNERS!

Seconds after the break-time bell rang, dozens of little monsters poured out from their classrooms and onto the playground. Two of the monsters moved faster than all the rest.

Just like they did every day, Som and Lilla were racing for the best toy on the playground—the golden hula hoop.

"That hula hoop is mine!" yelled Lilla.

"Not if I get there first!" Som shouted back, shoving her way past the other students. Then, suddenly—

PHWWWWWT!

The shriek of the playground supervisor's whistle stopped Som in her tracks.

Uh oh. The supervisor, Mrs. Mel, was headed straight for Som.

"Hello, Som," Mrs. Mel said. "What's the big rush? Why were you pushing the other monsters?"

"After you have said sorry to everyone, we can go and ask Lilla to share the hula hoop. Monsters with good manners apologize when they do something wrong."

Once Som said sorry to everyone she had pushed, she and Mrs. Mel went to Lilla together.

"Som would like to share the hula hoop with you," Mrs. Mel said. Som nodded.

Lilla looked confused. "We can't both hula hoop at the same time," she said.

"Not at the same time," Mrs. Mel chuckled. "You can take turns."

"Oh... " said Lilla. "I guess we could."

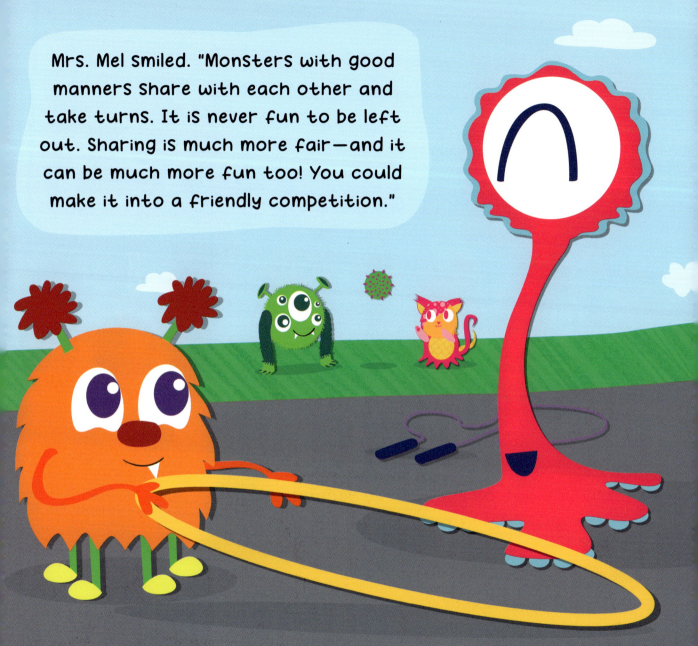

Mrs. Mel smiled. "Monsters with good manners share with each other and take turns. It is never fun to be left out. Sharing is much more fair—and it can be much more fun too! You could make it into a friendly competition."

Lilla and Som liked that idea.

Mrs. Mel helped Som and Lilla count how many seconds each of them could spin the hula hoop for.

Som was out of breath. "50 seconds for you, and 43 seconds for me. That's my best ever!"

"Well done!" said Lilla. "Mrs. Mel is right. Taking turns is much more fun than hula hooping alone."

PHWWWWWT!

When Mrs. Mel's whistle went off again, it wasn't to scold the little monsters—it was to tell them that break time was over.

"Make sure you put all the equipment back where it belongs," Mrs. Mel called. "Remember, monsters with good manners clean up after themselves."

The monsters worked together to clean the playground up. All the equipment went back into the correct boxes. All the trash went into the garbage.

Before they went inside, Som smiled at Lilla. "Let's play together again after school," she said.

"Yes, let's," Lilla agreed.

The park was very busy. There were so many little monsters at the playground that every single piece of equipment was being used.

Before anyone could stop him, little Rokko had run over to a monster called Goob. Goob was enjoying the swing.

"Me go! Me go!" said Rokko.

"Rokko!" Som and Lilla called, running after him. Som took her brother's hand and took him to the side.

"Rokko, you can't push people to get what you want—that's bad manners," Som explained.

"Let's show our good manners and say sorry together," Lilla said.

Som and Lilla took little Rokko back to the swing. "I'm sorry for pushing you," Rokko said.

"That's alright," Goob said. "Thanks for coming over to say sorry."

"When you are finished on the swing, please could we have a turn?" Som asked. "Rokko loves swings!"

"Sure!" said the monster. "I have to go soon anyway. That's my mom over there. She is waiting for me."

Som and Lilla looked where the monster was pointing.

They were surprised to see a familiar face...

"Mrs. Mel!"

"Your mom is Mrs. Mel?" Lilla asked.

"Yes—but I just call her mom," the monster said, waving at his mom. Mrs. Mel came over.

"Hello, pet. Hello, Som and Lilla," she said. "Are you all playing nicely?"

"Yes, we are," they all said.

"Mom, Som and Lilla have such good manners," Goob said. "They are even teaching their little brother to have good manners too."

"That's wonderful," Mrs. Mel said with a proud smile. "Well done, girls."

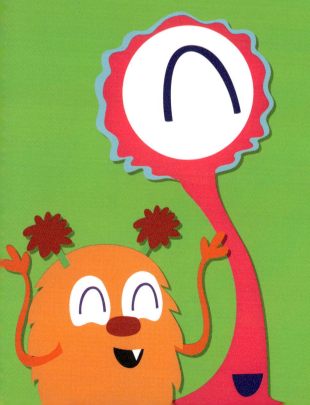

Not all monsters have good manners, but Som and Lilla do. Do you?

Can you remember the playground manners?

- Never push, shove, hit, or kick anyone.
- Use kind words.
- Say sorry if you do something wrong.
- Share and take turns.
- Clean up after yourself.